P9-CLR-704

THE ANIMAL TRAIL

Four Seasons of Wildlife Photography • Manabu Miyazaki

Chronicle Books • San Francisco

First published in the United States 1988 by Chronicle Books

Animal Trails in Four Seasons was first published by Heibonsha,
Limited, Publishers, Tokyo. Copyright © 1986 by Manabu Miyazaki.
All rights reserved. No part of this book may be reproduced in any
form without written permission from Chronicle Books.
Printed in Japan by Dai Nippon Printing Co., Tokyo.
Library of Congress Cataloging-in-Publication Data
Miyazaki. Manabu, 1949–
    The Animal Trail
    Translation of: Kemonomichi no shiki.
    1. Zoology—Japan—Japanese Alps—Pictorial works. 2. Seasons—
Japan—Japanese Alps—Pictorial works. I. Title.
QL325.M57313   1988   599.0952'1   87-24282
ISBN 0-87701-430-2 (pbk.)

Editing: Charles Robbins
Composition: On Line Typography
Cover design: Karen Pike

Distributed in Canada by
Raincoast Books
112 East Third Avenue
Vancouver, B.C.
V5T 1C8
10   9   8   7   6   5   4   3   2   1

Chronicle Books
San Francisco, California

THE ANIMAL TRAIL

Many small, mysterious communities of animals are nestled amid the hills bordering our towns and the woods shading our homes, their lives a complex web of seasonal cycles, mutual needs, and unwavering patterns. Over the centuries, these creatures have adapted to many changes in their habitats, but the recent, persistent encroachments of human beings have given them their most difficult test. The arrival of humans displaces animals and birds, replacing forests with houses, trails with highways, and flowers with parking lots. The familiar routines and timeless relationships often give way under the weight of human demands.

The problem is particularly acute in Japan where people are constantly moving into remote, peaceful regions formerly inhabited only by animals. Even the creatures of the Japanese Alps must bear the intrusions of civilization.

For many years I have been intrigued by the wild animals of Japan's high mountains. Their lives and habits are still puzzling, and I have spent many happy hours trying to capture on film the essence of their wildness.

I devised a robot camera equipped with an infrared sensor and placed it on a mountain trail at 4,500 feet to record the region's animal population. The small creatures made extensive use of a path originally trampled out by mountain climbers, and most displayed admirable nonchalance in front of the camera. They were like actors without fear of the camera as they threaded their way along the mountain trail.

I was pleased to have discovered a method for improving our knowledge of those animals and, at the same time, anxious to learn more. I wanted to observe the variations in animal behavior caused by the actions of people. Eventually, I decided to begin a project to photograph the creatures near human habitations and in close contact with civilization.

My own house provided the ideal setting. Located in the Indinai Valley, surrounded in the east by the Southern Alps and in the west by the Central Alps, it is midway up the mountains at about 3,000 feet. The building is distant from heavy concentrations of people, but various farms, inns, and vacation homes are scattered around the area. Towering above this gentle landscape are the majestic, snow-capped peaks.

From a nearby larch forest, foxes, badgers, and weasels frequently make forays to my garden. Their activities raised questions about their reaction to humans and their willingness to tolerate intrusions into their territory.

Investigation revealed that those animals relied upon an intricate trail system leading from garbage pit to garbage pit, from peach trees to corn patches, from watermelon fields to fish ponds. And their actions were coordinated with the lives of the people sharing their mountain valley.

Having decided to set up a series of robot cameras, I needed first to determine which trails were most heavily used and which most likely to yield worthwhile plates. By tying small pieces of string at various strategic spots and heights, I was able to select a site for the first camera based upon the number of times the strings were disturbed by passing animals.

One site about a quarter of a mile from my home was heavily used. The area supported many animals, and I soon learned that they were active on both sides of the stream that meandered through the forest. The animals repeatedly crossed the water on a log wedged between the banks. On the map this is location A, the center of summertime activity. However, during the winter, they crossed further downstream by hopping over snow-covered rocks at location C.

Seemingly isolated as it twisted through the larch grove, the trail was actually surrounded by many buildings and a busy highway. It offered an ideal locale for the cameras. In fact, despite the proximity of humans, the trail appeared quite remote, its overhanging larches and lush carpet of grass muffling the distant sounds of humanity. The burbling stream, the inquisitive birds, and the swift, soft-footed forest creatures thrived in a land of calm beauty.

Despite the cars and the people, the animals evidently relied heavily on the trail, so I situated that first camera about ten feet from the stream on flat land among the larches. The trees were planted about thirty years ago and trimmed periodically.

Thus the view is often unobstructed for many yards, and, I believe, this absence of heavy vegetation encouraged the animals, since they could easily survey the land, unhindered by dense foliage. This open landscape made them less vulnerable to predators. From my point of view, the location was ideal because the road is only 100 feet away and is heavily used during the summer by picnickers and campers.

Positioned in February of 1982, that first camera is still operating. We had a light snowfall that year which added to the success of the experiment because the animals were able to move freely even during the winter months.

At the same time, I placed a second camera across the water and about 700 feet from the first at location D. The land here is slightly higher than at the first spot and is punctuated by many rocks. During that initial year, I obtained very satisfactory results: fourteen different species of mammals and twelve varieties of birds passed before the camera.

After one year, I decided to reposition the second camera another 150 feet away, simply to take advantage of a field of wild butterburs that I knew would make a beautiful backdrop when they blossomed in May. Over the months of the experiment, this third location was very productive in terms of the large number of animals captured on film.

The movements of these animals were naturally dependent upon the cycles of the seasons and the productivity of nature. I was impressed by the vitality of the plant world. In early summer, the plants seemed to compete in shooting out new leaves, and my camera often recorded overnight growth of six to twelve inches. I had to be especially attentive to the equipment, for often a weed would shoot up at night, repeatedly triggering the camera as the plant waved back and forth in the breeze.

Throughout the years of observation, the animals moved in habitual ways, their lives tied to the vagaries of weather and food. Winter reduced the number of photographs, but, surprisingly, the months of July and August were also periods when there were fewer animals. I believe the proliferation of grass and plants in those months made the animals more cautious. Since they could not see far in the dense underbrush, they had to be more deliberate to avoid predators. Then too, many mammals migrated to the higher mountains in summer, returning to the valley only after the onset of autumn.

Larger animals such as Japanese serows and monkeys were not unduly troubled by the dense vegetation. On the other hand, hares and most small creatures stayed in the patches of open ground, matching their feeding habits to the flourishing plant life.

The most frequently observed animals were raccoon dogs. Not true raccoons, these relatives of the fox are named for the black patch around their eyes, similar in shape to that of a raccoon. Their appearance near the village was not surprising as they have long been known to favor the land around human habitations. In fact, the Chinese character for raccoon dog signifies an animal associated with human village life.

Hares were the next most photographed mammal, followed distantly by weasels and badgers. Though occupying a large territory, weasels appeared only in spring and early summer, then they disappeared until making a brief visit in early autumn. Badgers were very active. After a long winter hibernation, they made daily and nightly treks, generally traveling in pairs.

One badger couple in particular was easy to spot because the male suffered from alopecia, a disease that causes loss of hair on certain parts of the body. Badgers were never intimidated by the camera and shared this brashness with weasels and sables.

However, raccoon dogs and foxes, members of the dog family, possess excellent memories and were nervous around the cameras. After being startled once by the flash, they would not visit the same locale for several months.

Despite the minor limitations of the cameras and the reluctance of some animals to be photographed, I have been well pleased with the robot equipment. It offers an objective, candid glance into the silent realms of nature and a quick glimpse at the intriguing existence of the animals that share our lives.

I learned much that was hitherto unknown about wildlife. Most astonishing—and most pleasing—were the many varieties and large numbers of animals. Furthermore, despite popular wisdom that holds these creatures disappear once people invade their territories, it is obvious they have adapted well to the existence of human beings and continue to live in close, secret harmony on the fringes of our settlements.

My work has opened new levels of understanding, and I am resolved to continue the project in order to photograph and study other areas of Japan. In this way, I hope to ease the way for cooperation between humans and animals and to broaden people's knowledge of the world we share with the animals.

The Equipment

The photography equipment consists of an infrared phototube, a camera, and a stroboscope. When the infrared beam of the phototube is broken, the stroboscope and camera are triggered. A simple idea, it requires careful adjustment in the field to function properly.

Electricity was supplied by automobile batteries, a reliable source of low cost, outdoor energy needing only occasional recharging. The camera and light were housed in acrylic boxes similar to those used for underwater photography. Those watertight housings assured perfect protection for the equipment as well as efficient performance throughout the years of the experiment. To record the time of each shot, I placed a small digital clock so it was photographed with each opening of the camera lens.

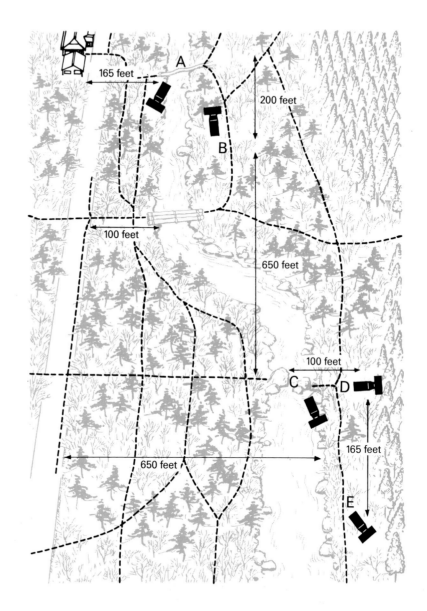

A Convenient Crossing

Carried by snow melt from the high mountains,

this log has wedged between the banks, forming an excellent bridge

used frequently by small animals.

During the spring and early summer, weasels were the most
active animals along the stream and were constantly dash-
ing across the makeshift bridge.

Despite their size, badgers also utilized the small log. This
sturdy hunter makes a hurried night crossing.

A raccoon dog tries the icy bridge. Not true raccoons, these
relatives of the fox are named for the raccoon-like black
patch around their eyes. Dormant during heavy snows, these
animals soon dig themselves out of their dens to seek food.

5

This view emphasizes the open, wooded terrain of the valley.

In the Larch Grove

After winding along the stream,

the trail bumps abruptly over a larch root that is

camouflaged by the lush undergrowth.

The bubbling stream nearby masked the camera's noise and
muffled the sounds of passing animals.

An alert hare takes an evening stroll, its pathway curtained
by masses of yellow flowers.

Another midnight visitor freezes before the camera; the
hare's ability to remain undetected is its best defense against
a threat.

Left: One of more than thirty raccoon dogs in the area, this vigilant creature tramps a familiar thoroughfare in the night woods.

Above: Aggressive young raccoon dogs often challenge their elders for rights to the trail, but they are usually ignored by the more experienced animals which see no benefit in fighting over a few yards of dirt.

People gathering edible plants shared the trails with neighborhood animals.

Right: A high-spirited weasel scurries home, its small prey clutched in strong jaws.

Siberian meadow buntings were but one of the many
species of birds to pass before the cameras.

Numerous jays were attracted to the effulgent yellow
blossoms.

Many stray cats stalked these trails but seldom lingered in the area.

The badger's distinctive eye mask is prominent in this
photograph taken on an early May morning.

A female monkey and her baby moving toward the valley
from the mountains. Note the heavy foliage that has grown
in the two years since the camera was first emplaced.

A bounding hare triggers the ever-vigilant camera.

Ferocious and agile hunters, weasels such as this rain-soaked climber often raid birds' nests for eggs.

Right: In three years, this particular camera only caught one fox—the animals are simply too intelligent to be tricked more than once.

Although considered quite rare, two albino raccoon dogs lived in the neighborhood but, perhaps because they sensed they were more conspicuous, were more cautious around people than their darker cousins.

Left: Seen in pairs during the spring and autumn, these raccoon dogs sport luxuriant coats of fur in preparation for the coming winter.

In July the camera caught an adult masked palm civet, but not until the following Christmas did another member of that species appear.

24

In December, this young civet loitered for about ten days.
Photographed on two separate nights, it was never satisfied
by its investigation of this larch.

Right: The single appearance of a bullheaded shrike, a rare
occurrence that seemed to presage a severe winter.

Because the book's photos are arranged not chronologically but to convey a sense of the entire trail and its seasonal changes, this shot of a hare, the first snapped in this location, is a good benchmark for tracing the changes in the trail.

28

Taken shortly after the previous photo, in March, this
features one of the many raccoon dogs that were particularly
active and playful as winter softened into spring.

During the fishing season, many anglers also used the trails.

Left: A Japanese serow, sometimes called a goat-antelope, traversed the trail regularly to circle the village.

The view overlooking the stream.

The Community of Animals

Day and night, the trail was in constant

use, the time of day and the seasons playing their part

in altering the animals' routines.

Weasels appeared in this location only from April through
June, but, interestingly, no females were ever photographed.

White hares were very rare. Because the winters at this
elevation are relatively mild, few hares completely change
their coats during that season.

Caught in stop-action as it scampered through the bushes,
this hare presents a fine view just as it starts a power-
ful spring.

35

Because of the terrain, many pheasants, such as this female with its young, lived in the area, yet I never sighted a male bird.

Chinese bamboo partridges were the most numerous birds, but, unlike pheasants, both parents usually accompanied the young.

At least three groups of monkeys totaling about seventy animals inhabit the foot of the Alps. These were part of a long line ambling down the trail.

Left: A Japanese macaque munches the leaves of a kudzu plant.

39

The land in this area is a game reserve, so I suspect this hunter was assigned specifically to thin the overbred hare population.

Left: The great majority of the monkeys on the trail were young adults with youngsters. The older animals apparently preferred a different route.

Left: Occasionally, the trail can become crowded, as this raccoon dog discovered one night when a bat whizzed overhead.

Above: Martens, close relatives to badgers, were rarely seen because they tend to remain on the higher slopes, away from human dwellings.

This serow had lost part of its horn, an important instrument and symbol of courtship, and, therefore, it retreated to the lower valley, seemingly ostracized by its fellows.

Ambushed by light and camera, this sly, quick hunter will
not soon return to this location.

Many field mice inhabit this area, but only in winter, when
their paths were raised closer to the cameras' height by
snow, was I able to photograph the lively creatures.

Few squirrels were seen. This little one was observed only once and may have been taken later by one of the predatory birds nesting nearby.

The bright and sunny landscape was home to many jays which frolicked during the day, unconcerned about the camera.

48

Crows clustered around the neighboring houses, but these
intelligent birds were difficult to capture on film because
they quickly spotted the concealed camera.

During one mild winter, six or seven common buzzards (hawks) wintered here, undoubtedly drawn by the abundance of field mice.

50

One camera was located here in some dense foliage.

A Ring of Bright Flowers

Climbing gently above a low cliff, the

trail here is brightly lighted during the day and supports many

types of plants along its borders.

This hare, captured in mid-jump, was but one of many
using this heavily traveled path.

This serow passed the same spot for three years as it moved toward a forest of Japanese cypresses. They are solitary animals, and not until this one died was another serow seen in the area.

54

The single visit by a Himalayan black bear was startling
since it was daytime and many people were about, but the
ripe raspberries were a temptation difficult to resist.

Another fisherman moving along the stream.

Left: This badger couple made frequent appearances. The second has alopecia, a disease that causes loss of fur.

Scampering at top speed, this marten was filmed in one
one-thousandth of a second.

Very proud and clever, this albino raccoon dog is out, even
in winter, to search for food.

In winter, this rocky crossing became the main crossing
point of the stream.

The Winter Way

Used only in winter, this ford required

concentration, for a single mistake could send the careless

plunging into freezing water.

A fox deftly leaps the frozen rocks.

Following pages: Martens also used the crossing, easily jumping from stone to stone.

Uncharacteristically clumsy, this monkey has just made the
distant bank and barely avoided a cold bath.

With their short legs, raccoon dogs are less agile than foxes
and would often patiently walk the banks, seeking a suitable
crossing point.

Primarily ground dwellers, Chinese bamboo partridge also
used the rocks but wisely elected to use wings instead of feet
when negotiating the stream.